Social Engagement

Growing your Young Living team,
network, & lifestyle using social media.

By MAGGIE TONG
with Life Science Publishing

TABLE OF CONTENTS

INTRODUCTION

I love socializing. I love sharing. I even feel great when I get up to speak—not many people would say that. Even better, I love meeting new people, getting to know them, and ultimately, helping them.

Now, many people will tell you that social media is a one-to-many tool that they build their lives around, but I'm here to say that it's something altogether different. It's actually a great one-to-one tool that brings you closer together, when used correctly. Your life shouldn't be centered around social media. Your social media should be centered around your life.

This book is called *Social Engagement* for a reason. Social engagement doesn't mean social media necessarily. It means making a real connection—not just sending glorified advertisements out to the world. It means truly engaging with another person—whether you are doing this one-on-one or in a group setting.

When I met my husband, Hill Ngan, we got engaged. We didn't just start advertising to each other. We connected. We engaged with one another so we could get engaged to be married.

Engagement takes on a huge meaning when it comes to social media. It's not about how many posts you send out to the world. It's about touching lives, one-by-one.

I am a 38-year-old mom from Hong Kong with two young girls, and I happen to have a successful Young Living business—one that I'm very proud of. But, it's taken years of study and dedication to get there.

I started my first business with my husband (then boyfriend) when I was 22. Before I started doing business, the Internet was already a big part of my life (and subsequently became a part of my business later on). When I was 19 — I created my first website. Since then, I have enjoyed sharing my daily lives and interests. I think I was in the first wave of young people that created personal websites. For me, everything was self-taught — from the website interface, to guestbooks, to writing some simple scripts. You don't need to be exceptional to do it. YOU can do it too.

Just remember this: you have the power to learn just about anything you put your mind to and give a little effort. You have a best friend—and its name is Google. There's a video tutorial on just about everything these days. So as I start giving you ideas about social engagement, it's up to you to engage with it and take next steps!

WHY BE SOCIAL?

We learn and grow through being social. Our first lessons with our parents were our introduction to being social.

As you share your Young Living lifestyle, the products actually speak for themselves. People will join your team when they see you using the products. With the rise of several social media platforms, this is easier to do than ever.

It's all about the experience. Social media helps you explore new ways to help people have an experience with oils.

People have always bought in a personal way. A little over a hundred years ago, that's the only way people purchased things—person to person. It makes sense that we buy from people we like.

Relationships of any kind really depend on trust. For all of humankind's previous generations, this depended on location and custom. Now things are different. Our global community thrives on the fact that someone in Hong Kong can not only communicate with someone in Omaha, Nebraska, but also be friends—even if they've never met.

BEING SOCIAL

Social media is exactly what it says: it's social. It's about being personal and creating a relationship. People won't come to Facebook to see your oils. They will come to your Website, Facebook page, or Twitter feed to hear stories, watch DIYs, share experiences, ask questions, and look for new ideas. They'll spend time with you if you help them take care of their health, care for their families, save money, save time, feel better, and feel happier.

That's why I never sell the compensation plan. I never sell the products. Instead, I tell stories. When people come to me with a question, I focus on helping them get the answer they need. It's pretty simple, right?

You can distill it into a little equation:

> Specialized audience
> + Valued content + Genuine caring
>
> = A Big Young Living Business

THE EARLY YEARS

Before I get into the social media details, let me offer a little background on how my own experience with business and the Internet grew into what it is today.

At that time, I shared on my homepage a collector doll named Blythe. Some people think it's a weird looking doll, but nonetheless it gained huge popularity in Hong Kong. I would post interesting articles and nice photos to humanize the doll.

If you write about something that is trending, the Internet will naturally bring you a lot of hits. Chances are, people are looking it up on search engines already. Writing about Blythe brought me a lot of followers and a sizable audience. I then started designing my own Blythe doll clothes, and people became interested in buying them. Within 2 months, I was able to turn the sales of Blythe doll clothes into an actual business.

A DOLL NAMED BLYTHE

I started my first factory, a small one with 20 workers. It was more like a studio actually. It was for making Blythe clothes for my own brand. The Blythe trend was started by a Japanese company, it was extremely popular in Japan. I applied to attend the Blythe exhibition in Japan (I didn't speak Japanese and asked a friend for help) and exhibited the clothes that I made there.

I always made great sales that were enough to cover my cost plus a little extra. So, some Japanese companies started reaching out to me such as Hobby Japan, a company that has toy stores in every PARCO Department store in Japan. They quickly became my exclusive reseller in Japan. I was very proud of this achievement.

A lot of Japanese who are Blythe enthusiasts knew about me as well. I was only 23 at that time. Blythe also became popular in the United States because of a photographer named Gina Garan. Gina was a distributor of my products in the U.S. as well, and I had many customers there.

My studio slowly grew in size and became a small factory (40-50 workers). Other than doing clothes for my own brand, I accepted other orders as well. When there is a trend, it's easy for you to ride the trend and grow exponentially in size in a short period of time. But once the trend is over, and things become out of date (Young Living does not go out of date though!), things can shrink just as quickly. At the same time, my nose allergy was becoming very bad especially because I always had to work with fabrics in the factory. So this was the second time my dad had ever told me to quit a job. He suggested that I could help him in his company. But I turned down his offer, and decided to move forward with my kidswear business instead. It was a critical moment of my career.

BECOMING A MOM

Conclusion: Successful people believe in themselves. They are proactive.

A few years after doing this business, I gave birth to my first child. I started blogging about her growth in my website. My main purpose was just to document the daily life of my daughter, and I put a lot of effort in it. I also wanted to help other new moms as an ally with my tips and experiences. It was a platform for us to motivate each other. Other than a website and a blog, I also started a forum to share parenting tips. It became a place where people could chat and share their own experiences daily.

MOM FACEBOOK FACTOR

In December of 2007, I started my Facebook account. A lot of my friends had Facebook accounts so I started one too, and I started sharing my life on Facebook.

When I first started all this, my intention was purely to share my personal interests. It had nothing to do with making money or anything business related. In my blog, I documented:

- my daughter's growth
- where I took her to play
- personal parenting tips I found helpful
- how to dress her up and take nice pictures
- even my cooking recipes

In 2008, I started my Facebook page (named after my business - CCK). It became a new platform for people (in the forum) to chat with each other. When I first started all this, my intention was purely to share my personal interests.

Quickly, people started noticing her clothes and asked where I had bought them. At this time, I thought of another business opportunity — I could have my own kids wear certain brands and be ambassadors. Actually, that HAD BEEN my dream for a long time. So I started planning it, and I opened my first CCK shop in November of 2008. Because of my existing network and fan base through my blog, my shop became popular immediately. Within 3 years, I opened 8 shops in Hong Kong. By sharing these stories, I want to bring one idea across:

If you sincerely put your heart into sharing good information with your audience,
even if you are not thinking about how it would benefit you initially,
it could become a pleasant surprise later on. You never know.

THE COST OF PRIVACY

Back in my first years I preferred putting content outside of my own domain (my own website) because I felt much more secure. But then I realized that the public domain was (and is) more easily searchable, and it could increase a site's popularity through the ranking systems. So, I quickly moved my content to a Yahoo blog. If you still think that you want to keep your content in your own domain, you may want to reconsider.

BLOGGING—A NATURAL ADVERTISER

So blogging became a part of my life. It was how I found I could share my interests. There was no sponsorship for bloggers back then, everything that I shared on my blog, I had paid for out-of-pocket.

For example, I shared my experience of taking my daughters to Disneyland, the kind of chocolate I like to eat, advice on how I cured my allergy, traveling, crafting, fashion. At the beginning, everything I shared had to do with my own interests.

As time went on, I discovered opportunities for enjoying the things I liked while being subsidized for my endorsement. Through my blogging efforts I became an Ambassador for Disney. They invited me to their social media "mom" conference in Florida, which was fully sponsored. My favorite chocolate brand, Godiva, sends me chocolate all the time. My favorite jewelry brand, Thomas Sabo, sponsors me as well—sending me samples and freebies.

Because of the posts I wrote about my allergy, Dyson gave me a vacuum cleaner. Trollbeads, a jewelry brand, sponsored me as well and sent some great pieces.
Initial, a fashion brand from HK, is my sponsor as well. Because I had shared about my traveling experiences, The Luxe Nomad starting sponsoring some trips as well.
All of this was truly unexpected and came as a pleasant surprise.

The peak of my kidswear clothing business was in 2010, after my second daughter was born, and continued until 2013. Whether it was my clothing brand, or blogging influences, these two things brought many benefits to my family. At one point, I think I could safely say I was the number one parenting blogger in HK.

MONETIZING THROUGH SPONSORSHIP

Every time a company approaches me for sponsorship, I consider many factors. I take into account their reputation and the quality of their products. I ask, "are they suitable for my audience(s)? What benefit(s) will this partnership give me? What would I have to lose? Would I be trading one sponsorship for another that might come into conflict?"

I see that many bloggers just accept whatever sponsors come to them. In reality, actually doing so can quickly burn your reputation. I built a really strong trust between my fan base and me. It's something I take seriously and never squander on shady products or questionable sponsors.

TRUST & YOUR FAN BASE

In 2013, I published my first parenting book, Candy Dream. It's actually semi-autobiographically about my life story, my relationship with my husband, parenting, family travel, Disney, and allergies. Within half a year, all 3000 books were sold out. (For Hong Kong, that is quite a good number.)

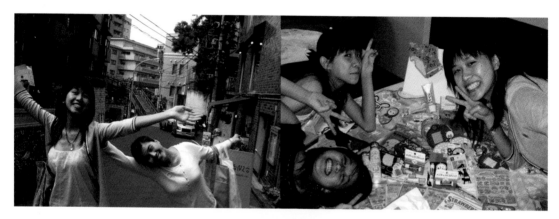

PASSION WILL DRIVE YOU FORWARD

I always enjoyed what I did. I was making quite a good income at that time. But with success, also came the haters. They will disagree with what you do — which is natural, everyone has a different perspective. But on the Internet, people always go to the very extreme in criticizing other people. That made me want to step back, because I didn't want to involve my children in this. They're not babies anymore. I didn't want them to be affected by this.

It's a tough day when you realize that the Internet is not such an innocent place. I still used the network I built for my clothing business. I did this just to make a living. I stopped sharing my private life, and my influences slowly came down.

Actual audiences don't like when you sell stuff. They want to read about REAL life. But to me at the time, my network was just my tool to make money. Additionally, because the economy wasn't doing well, my business was trending downward. It was still good, but not expanding like it once was.

When you have a business that isn't doing increasingly better, it becomes a source of pressure and stress.

So, if you are reading this book today looking to be a successful blogger with lots of sponsors that will help you make money off your efforts, you bought the right book because the tools are here.

However, making money from blogging at any cost is your actual strategy, it will not be long lasting. It's not as happy of a thing as you might imagine. Keep in mind as well that I have 16 years of successful retail business experience. Even so, I chose not to continue in the end. What I will say is it's best to use social media to help extend your MLM network, and bring you sustainable, successful financial freedom.

BLOGGING

The good: You get sponsored, sometimes with expensive products. You get paid to write. A lot of blogger events extend your network, and broaden your horizon. When you accept a campaign, you have to learn more about it and you learn stuff.

The bad: You become commercialized and your audiences can tell. Every time you do it you are potentially burning your reputation. You charm your way back into the hearts of your audience, but it becomes increasingly difficult. If you do JUST this for a living, it's hard to do it well and not become completely commercialized. Haters will attack you.

TRADITIONAL BUSINESS

The good: Flexible time. Opportunities are much more than working for a company. You can do what you like. Very rewarding.

The bad: Big investment. High risk. Hours could be long. In a retail business the rent is expensive. You have to manage HR. You are affected by the ups and downs of the local, national, and global economy. Income is unstable.

YOUNG LIVING

The good: Improve health of friends and family. Expand your circle. Flexible working hours. The bigger your business grows, the fewer hours you work. The cost is extremely low (you only have to buy a Basic Starter Kit, or Premium Starer Kit, dependign on your market). You don't have to stock products out-of-pocket (which is usually a business cost). Free traveling. Your business could be inherited (Some MLM companies don't allow that). You could even sell your account to someone. Personal growth is fast.

The bad: I cannot think of anything bad. Can you?

WHICH ACCOUNTS TO OPEN

Next chapter: If you know nothing about social media, I will suggest you open some social media accounts.

It's a platform that's changing all the time. You don't have to force yourself to keep updated (e.g. Snapchat). You can start by using your geological advantage, meaning, think about what's popular in your region. For your area, is it Instagram? Facebook? You could also learn about new platforms like Snapchat, but you also need to learn what kinds of people use these platforms (Are they young people? Are they your target age group etc.?).

Instagram is very simple. There's no differentiation between a personal account and a fan page.

Facebook is more complicated and multi-functional. There's a strong differentiation between personal accounts, fan pages, and groups. But also because of these multi-functions, it helps you reach people outside your network. You can control the level of privacy to fit your needs. This time, I mainly want to talk about Facebook and how it helps you build your network.

1) A Personal Facebook Account allows you to share your private life within your friends circle. But if you are doing YL business, your personal Facebook is part of your personal branding.

2) Many people want to know how to reach outside of their existing network, and you can do this through Facebook pages. But a lot of people have the misconception that opening a Facebook page is a good idea. They think it'll help them sign up new members. Personally, I don't think that's a good way to do it, because a truly successful social media account will bring you more followers and reach new audiences in a very short time. If you are setting up a page to sell product (such as is the case with an MLM like Young Living), your audience will potentially lose trust. They will just see you as a stranger. You're just another online vendor.

THE POWER OF A THEME

When you want to start social media, you need to think about a theme of your page. Choose an overarching concept that incorporates everything you will want to post on such as parenting, cooking, beauty, sports, yoga, etc. Remember, you start with something that is not directly related to selling product right off the bat.

Some people never show their faces on their page. That's wrong, too. No matter how good your articles or witticisms or personal takes on a topic are, it's hard for your audience to build a relationship with you. Showing your face will humanize you. That is very important. That's how you build trust.

Always remember that you must reply to the comments. Don't think you're just replying to one comment. That's the wrong approach. You are actually building relationships with ALL of your audience members. People in your audience don't simply read what you are posting and ignore the rest. They read the comments too! In fact, a majority of people LOVE reading the comments.

No matter what kind of account you choose to use—personal Facebook, Facebook page or Facebook group—photo quality is VERY, VERY important. If you take bad photos, you're going to have to change that. You're going to have to learn how to take better photos. There are so many free tutorials on the web. Please, please, please, take at least 5 different free mini-courses to get yourself up to speed on beautiful photography. Pay attention to everything—reading your light and angle, capturing the photo, editing the photo, and getting the best from each and every photo you post.

YOUR THEME

I have mentioned this before, but it bears repeating. Whatever theme you pick for your page, you should try to pick something that is trending. You should choose something that is popular right now, something that feels current. This is huge, because it will help you increase your exposure to different audiences. And attracting a wide following is something that should be your primary concern.

It's hard to do something good if you don't like it. Behind every successful page is a good storyteller. Even though some pictures might not be interesting, they can be infinitely transformed by the right caption or commentary. An interesting caption can make all the difference.

Don't post randomly. Make sure all your posts are of good quality.

When you are doing a page, DON'T EVER rush to sell product, because that will damage your chance to build trust with your audience. Posts that are interactive are good (e.g. ask them a question or invite them to share advice).

Day by day, as your followers increase, you should start analyzing what kind of content they like. You need to come up with posts that are relatable. Look at the posts that get the most hits, the most likes, the most re-shares, the most people reached.

For example, I am a mom. I am a parenting blogger. Whatever I post needs to be relatable to moms. It needs to have an emotional appeal. Before I had kids, I never thought I could sacrifice everything for someone. This is something about which ALL MOMS will agree. You will make them feel as though you are the same as them. They will instantly connect, so they will start listening to you. You don't have to be positive all the time. Sometimes when you have struggles, you can share that too. Just be sure to put a "silver lining" spin on everything. Be vulnerable. Before you know it, suddenly they're your friends. They might start comforting you or give you their advice. Now you're on track.

THE TROUBLE WITH BRAGGING...

You must be very humble, NEVER show off. Don't show something that people cannot attain. Because you will make people feel uncomfortable. Then they won't want to read what you write.

I have a few examples of what's relatable to people:
1. People like when you're sharing about your parents getting old etc.
2. Spending time with your kids, good moments
3. Spending quality time with your spouse, write about being grateful
4. Use new features, e.g. Mother's Day "thankful" reaction; Facebook live has new emojis. People like to see new technology

I suggest you make good use of "Live," because it's very real. A lot of people are afraid of going live, I suggest you start with a partner. Don't do it randomly. Plan ahead your key points for what you want to talk about. Make the live session short (within 5 min). If it's too long, and people miss it, they won't start over, unless it's less than 5 minutes long.

If you want to use the 'live" feature well, you need to promote it ahead well ahead of time. It's always a good idea to have interactions with your audience, mention their names so they feel respected.

When your page gains certain popularity, I want to say 1000 followers, you can start talking about your products, for me its essential oils. But NEVER SELL. Use the products in your own REAL life.

Don't just post a picture of the product and a product description. Try to only mention product information with hashtags, because it's more subtle and informational.

The best way to make people curious about the product or what you're doing, is going to events. Show FABULOUS pictures of the events with a story. Don't show pictures with the brand. Don't talk about the brand. You don't even need to show the brand. It'll make people even more curious.

ON PERSONAL BRANDING...

I talked about your personal account being your personal branding, especially if you started your MLM business. Many of your downlines and members will add you as a friend on FB, or you should add them. It's an easier way for you to get to know each other. Since people nowadays spend so much time on social media, seeing your pictures and your life in their feeds will plant you in their subconscious mind—it's like they already know you. It builds trust.

Other than doing personal branding in your page, you could also do it in your personal FB account. A lot of people don't like to interact with others on public pages. You could comment on your downline stuff (to show that you care), you could share about your family, and you could share more about your deeper feelings. It'll help your Facebook friends—especially new friends—learn more about you on a personal level.

Don't set all your posts to "public," if you are trying to build a relationship with your posts. If a person comes to you and wants to make a connection and they only see your public posts, it's hard for them to trust you. They might feel you are not being genuine or you don't trust them enough to be personal.

Pick a personal image that suits you, I recommend that you keep a positive and optimistic mindset most of the time. (But you don't need to be positive ALL the time. Because some people ARE negative, they assume an overly positive blog is fake.)

We're all sad sometimes. That's just human nature. Be willing to share what is frustrating you, but be sure to be respectful in the process. If you're going to say something negative, say it with a little humor. Say it self-deprecatingly. This is my mantra: BE REAL. BE HUMAN. BE RELATABLE.

HELP OTHERS

Serve people more if you can. Be subtle and humble though. Call for action, not to show off.

Have a good image. Use hashtags. For example, try #GreenMonday, #HealthyEating habits, #AnimalRights.

I use these examples, but remember you have to be careful. Don't EVER talk about politics, if you are trying to use social media for your business. It is a very sensitive topic, and everyone has different views. You can feel free to have a political stance in your private life, but don't post it on social media. More verbal wars are started with politics than with anything else. The same goes for religion. You can allude to your religion, you may eve mention your religion, but don't get into the details. Above all, definitely do not judge other religions.

Be humble by seeking others' advice and help. It'll make that person happy, too. Constantly improve yourself. Read more books. Learn new skills.

HOW TO USE FACEBOOK GROUPS...

Facebook groups are a good way to make your team more devoted and grow your team. When your organization starts to take shape, you can use Facebook groups to build a stronger team spirit. Always identify yourself by your team name, not by your upline's name. This is because people might not like your upline.

Your team is everyone in your downline. Since you are a part of your team, you're not really a part of your upline. It's more common to dislike a person, but not a team, because teams usually represent an ideology.

In order to have a good team image, have a good logo, have a good sense of calling (for us, it's "believe in joy and happiness and bringing them to others," feminism, women helping other women). And the "calling" should be common to everyone.

In a group, everyone can post. In a page, only you have the ability to post. You could post on behalf of your page, but that doesn't have the same effect. In your personal Facebook, you are repeating yourself. But in a group, EVERYONE can participate. People can share their testimonials or stories. It makes people feel like sharing is a natural thing. Through liking other posts or getting likes, people feel that they are helping others, and in the process they grow. This type of growth brings out the "leader" quality of someone. You can also team up to make events, do some interesting activities (such as a do-it-yourself DIY workshop, have dinner meet ups, etc.). In the process you learn about each other. Remember to take more photos, because it'll attract more people to join your team and your business — new blood. Constantly attracting new blood is an important aspect of your business.

THE TOOLBOX

There are several social media tools (platforms) you'll want to explore as you grow your team:

- Personal Website
- Blogs
- Facebook
- Instagram
- Twitter
- Google
- Pinterest
- YouTube
- RSS feeds

These are the basics. You can grow your team without them, but you can grow a far better team more quickly with them. But, you don't always have to use all of them to be successful. The important thing is to know what generally works with each one, and more importantly, uncover what works for you!

You may not like Twitter. But if you don't, you might miss out on a whole generation of people who live by it each and every day. You may love LinkedIn, but it may not help you find that audience of people who might want to try Young Living products. You might like having your classically-programmed Website, but find that it can't enable you to host a party or film a video and post it easily.

WHICH IS WHICH?

Who uses which social platform and why? Do you happen to like Twitter or Facebook more? What about Vine or Snapchat? How about Instagram or Pinterest? You might happen to like one more, but it really goes without saying that you try your hand at all of them.

It's difficult to determine which platform is best for your business if you don't know a thing about them or their strengths. The important thing is to give yourself room and opportunity to explore and experiment.

PLAY = SUCCESS

Social media platforms aren't difficult. If they were, then children who get ahold of their parents' accounts wouldn't be able to wreak such havoc! The important thing is to be willing to play around with the platform so that it really works like second nature for you.

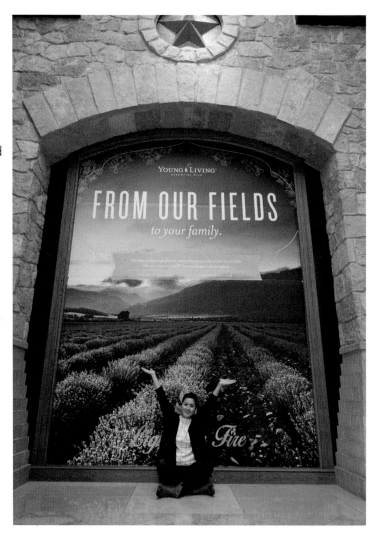

THE 3 KINDS OF PEOPLE WHO FAIL...

I always say there are three kinds of people who shouldn't try to grow a Young Living team. They are:

1. Negative people
2. Lazy people
3. People who don't use the products

But in the spirit of being positive, I'd rather turn that around and say there are three kinds of people who are bound to SUCCEED. They are:

1. Positive/optimistic
2. Ambitious/willing to work
3. Products of the product (people who use and like Young Living products)

CHOOSE GREAT IDENTITIES

When I say "identity" I really mean your online name, your website, your profile, your screen name. Put some thought into it. Be sure that it's easy for people to pick up on your humor or tie-in with your business. Keep things neutral.

MAKE EVERYTHING PRETTY

All of us know what it means to swipe left, right? Well, when it comes to things you post, that's what people are doing. When they stumble on your page, you have to have beautiful photographs. You have to have clean, gorgeous photography. Otherwise, in about 5 seconds or less, they'll move on.

In nearly every type of social media platform, you'll need a personal picture. Take some time to choose a really good one. Try to keep the same picture in all of your personal branding. After all, you're not Cher. (Or, maybe you are. In that case, "Hi, superstar!") You're not trying to be 10 completely different looking people in the space of an hour performance. You never want people to get confused. There's so much noise in our daily lives that consistency has an advantage. You want them to see your best photo and instantly recognize you—anywhere they stumble onto you in the social universe.

GETTING TO BE A BETTER PHOTOGRAPHER

Try Templates

Knowing what you're going to do with a photo before you shoot it makes all the difference. Get a good idea for how creative photos are set up. One great way to do this is to check out stock photographs such as Shutterstock, Imagestock, StockSnap.io, or PhotoPin. Take a few test shots to get your bearings.

Daylight is Best

Your best photo friend could possibly be daylight. You can invest in a lighting kit or a DSLR, but that will take a lot of practice and study. It's much easier to find a great place that's bathed in natural sunlight. You might try an area near a window.

When you're inside, put your subject near a window, but don't put it in direct light. As you go outside, early evening or late morning daylight is less harsh. A bright cloudy day actually functions like a light box. On a bright, sunny day, wait for an opportune cloud to soften the light.

Seamless White

More often than not, you'll need something on a white background. Start with a great piece of white foam core. Place it near a light source (such as a window), but avoid direct sunlight. Stand over the object (careful to avoid shadows) and shoot it looking down. Sometimes, you might have to get up on a chair to get the best lighting and angle. Play with brightness and contrast in your photo editing and you should be good to go.

Shoot at least 25 photos of the object you want to capture. Try creating a "scene" for the object, try different angles, different distances from the object, and different lighting setups. Crop in so that the white field looks seamless.

Use a Selfie Stick

As corny as it sounds, selfie sticks are great for getting you that shot. You can study your angle, you can read the light, and you're not trusting your all-important shot to a random stranger that may or may not know how to take a good picture. There's always one that can fit in your purse, briefcase, or pocket.

Try Video

Sometimes the best photos come from video stills. Think about it. Many movie posters actually have been extracted from the real movie footage.

Edit, Edit, Edit

Shop every app or photo editing software in the book. There's a new one every day. Try all of the filters. Experiment with your photos, and make BIG adjustments. Pull the sliders all the way one way or the other to really get a feel for what you're doing. There are a million tutorials you can Google about the subject from YouTube to Vimeo.

THE TOP SIX DESKTOP PHOTO-EDITING TOOLS
(at the time of printing)

Adobe Photoshop

Photoshop is the big one, and you can have access to most of the features for as little as $9.99/month. You can work in layers, run filters, airbrush, modify lighting, adjust vibrance. The great news is that you can create template files to work from and create your edited photos much faster.

Canva

Canva is probably the most popular free online design tool that helps you finish professional-looking images. The great news about Canva is that they have over 1 million preexisting images and graphics you can choose from and blend them with your own. They have thousands of templates so you're not really starting from scratch, and they provide a lot of free icons and fonts. Even the premium account prices are reasonable.

PicMonkey

This is another highly popular online photo editing tool that has both free and pay options. The key with this one is that you can really sharpen an image or fix the exposure. They have great custom effects and image touch-up tools to whiten teeth, fix blemishes, remove red-eye, and even spray tan. Better yet, they have their own free tutorials.

Picktochart

This one is for making reports, presentations, and infographics. Lots of templates, and they are easily customizable. It's also really intuitive. You can put in your own data, create an infographic, and watermark it with your logo. Fabulous!

Pixlr

This is the great free Photoshop alternative. This requires a bit of exploration and experimentation, but the software is powerful. If you're familiar with Photoshop, you'll be a natural.

Venngage

Venngage enables you to create flyers, reports, infographics, and social media posts. There are different categories—beginner, intermediate and advanced—they use to determine the complexity of the infographic. They have drag-and-drop icons, backgrounds, templates. It saves your work on the fly, so you can rest easy as you work with it.

PHOTOS FOR FREE

Check out these sites for plenty of amazing free images:

- Pixabay
- Gratisography
- Unsplash
- Psychography
- Magdeleine
- Morgue File
- Kaboompics
- Death to the Stock Photo
- PicJumbo

20 TIPS FOR TAKING MORE INTERESTING PHOTOS

on your phone

1) Don't be afraid to edit.

2) Try attaching an external lens.

3) Experiment with negative space.

4) Find different perspectives.

5) Play with reflections.

6) Focus on one subject.

7) Focus on Symmetry.

8) Look for Repetitive Patterns.

9) Play with Color Blocking.

10) Avoid zooming in.

11) Capture small details.

12) Use natural light.

13) Experiment with creating abstracts

14) Try taking pictures of a group of people laughing.

15) Be non-conventional.

16) Catch people in interesting candids.

17) Use perspective lines such as staircases and streets.

18) Use your phone's camera gridlines to balance the shot.

19) Play with motion and blur.

20) Experiment with overlays or "multi-exposure" (blending two photos together).

- Afterlight
- VSCO Cam
- Photoshop Express
- Snapseed
- SKRWT
- Live Collage
- Foodie
- Camera+
- Mextures
- Enlight

- Facetune
- Visage Makeup Editor

TEST WHAT PEOPLE SEE

Sometimes our web browsers and phone interfaces paint a great picture of us, but we really don't see how our posts look to the outside world. It's a great idea to use "Go Incognito" on a Google window and look at our posts from time to time. That way, we aren't fooled into thinking something looks great when it doesn't look the same to other people.

TELL YOUR PERSONAL STORY

Whether you came to Young Living because your daughter had allergies, or because your grandmother was allergic to pain medicine and needed some form of relief, tell your story. Make it personal. Add your pets, your friends, your spouse, your children, and your family members. Include your passions. Tell people why you want to be a beacon of positive change in the world. Whatever compelled you to start a new way of life and a new business may be contagious. Gary Young's passion caught on for so many of us. Let it do the same for people who come in contact with you!

WHAT'S IN A POST?

There are many ways to approach drafting a post. Here are some great ideas to get your mind going:

Help People… (Give people tips they can use, cover topics that actually help make life easier, healthier, more fun, or more rewarding.)

Give Them What They Want… (When you go to a party, who do the people gravitate toward? What are they telling? What is the story?)

If You Can't Say Something Nice… (Have a sense of humor, stay positive, find the silver lining even when you complain.)

Tell a Real Story… (Make it coherent. Don't be over-flowery in the telling, but be sure to tell interesting, relatable, genuine stories.)

Bring Value… (Offer ideas, recipes, life hacks, true reviews of products.)

Who cares…(As you post, everything must be relevant, or have a purpose. Gary never made a blend for profit. Rather, he made each and every blend for a purpose. Do the same when you post. Ask yourself, "what's in it for them?" "How will this relate to their lives?" What frustrates them? What gives them hope?)

Get to the Point (or Tell The Long of It in a Short Time) (Be Concise) (You have 5-8 seconds).

Show 'em (images are 63% of social media) (videos are 32%).

Make 'em do SOMETHING. (Offer a challenge of some sort to attract, engage, and convert. Rather than a classical Call-To-Action/CTA, think about getting them to do one little thing that they will enjoy or experience to help them have a feeling/experience about oils.)

Wake Up and Smell the Oils. (As you experiment with your social media strategy, look at what you're doing…and confirm what's working or not working.)

Better Together. (Get linked up with like-minded individuals who are actively doing what you want to do. Who do you like to follow? Why? How are you similar?)

Find Your Voice. (The more of your personality you can infuse into your writing and posts, the more attractive you'll be to a reader. In other words, put a little makeup on your writing. Also, the more you practice, the more you'll find your own genuine voice coming through. This is important because in a social network, the process of engaging with people will often root out the false players. You're looking to present an authentic voice, authentic view of yourself, authentic view of oils, authentic view of your experience, and authentic view of the company.)

TO PLAN OR NOT TO PLAN...

That's the question. Some people like to plan the kinds of posts for each social media platform—and they like to do it months in advance. Other people fly by the seat of their pants and post constantly about the spontaneous things in their lives. The important thing is to post often, post across your platforms, tie them together, and feel authentic.

If you happen to be a person who likes to plan out your strategy into campaigns, by all means, have at it. In that case, have a look at these tools:

Free	**Paid**
Asana	Agora Pulse
Excel (mostly)	Airtable
ContentCal	Buffer
Crowdfire	CoSchedule
Google Docs	DivvyHQ
Stresslimit (WordPress plug-in)	Edgar
	Everypost
	Friends+Me
	Futurity
	Hootsuite
	Hopper HQ
	Hubspot
	Loomly
	MaySocial
	Post Planner
	Sendible
	Social Pilot
	Social Oomph
	Sprout Social
	Tailwind

IF YOU LOVE IT, RE-SHARE IT!

When you start to build up a following, you'll find people are interested in the things you like. When you truly see something you like from one of your friends, re-share it! It's a great way to boost the number of people in your following. These tips also help you to expand without a lot of extra effort:

- Use "Popular Pins" on Pinterest
- Explore Google "Circles"
- Try Twitter "Lists" (public & private)
- Use Google Search to find like-minded communities

3 WORDS FOR YOU: POSITIVE, POSITIVE, & POSITIVE

Even when you complain, you have to see the silver lining and turn the story. It's not only a great way to add entertainment and comedy, but it also inspires. When people walk away feeling better than when they found you, you're in! You don't have to paint an artificially rosy picture. Instead, you use a combination of sarcasm, irony, and self-deprecating humor to make it more positive. If you can finish on an uplifting note, you've still been able to be honest, but you've also been able to keep things looking up.

THANKFUL

Many times you'll be re-posting, re-tweeting, or re-sharing something from someone else. By being humble and giving those people proper thanks and credit, you gain a lot of social cache.

BRAVE

Standing up to social injustice and supporting the underdog are great ways to get positive attention. As long as you speak your mind respectfully, you'll find many people in the world who will agree with you. If they don't, be prepared to ward off the trolls and the mean folks. They'll try to rip you down. Keep a post up if you truly believe in its positivity. But if you're really taking heat, don't be afraid to pull it, disable it, or delete it.

RELEVANT

Really, who cares? I mean really? For real, who really cares? If your posts don't connect to what's current, what's happening in the world, what helps people in the world, then there's no point. Unless the point is entertainment. In which case, be sure to bring your best Oscar Wilde or Jimmy Fallon.

INTERESTING

Sometimes the oddities are what grab our attention. It's those odd twists on seemingly well-known topics that get people to look and stay in your subscriber base.

CONCISE

The shorter, the better. When it comes to attention spans, the world is getting fuller and fuller of short ones. What can you say in a 6-page long rant that you can't say in a catchy 140-character tweet?

PRETTY/CATCHY

Again, the point is to be eye-catching. This is a relative term. I know people who have some of the prettiest designer clothes in the world, but when they go to their closets, all they see is drab, because they tend to purchase the same things—no matter who made it! So everything just looks the same. To be catchy is to be unique but approachable. Be as clever as you can.

SMART

This means intellectual as well as witty. When you have both, it's a perfect storm! Laugh a little. Learn a lot. Use your smarts!

MULTILINGUAL

In Hong Kong, many of us speak three languages—Cantonese, Mandarin, & English. This opens up doors for us. It's simply a reality we face. With Young Living, think of all the other countries and people you can help if you post in more than one language—especially if you speak the languages equally well, or at least, conversationally well.

THE LOVERS & THE HATERS

In the spirit of being Positive, Positive, Positive, assume the best when people comment on your posts. In the world of social media, there are people who want to offend for no reason. Don't take the time to be offended. Remember this quote from Abraham Lincoln: "We should be too big to take offense and too noble to give it." If you keep this in mind, it helps you grow a thick skin—something you'll need for long-term survival in the world of social media.

AGREE TO DISAGREE

No two people will ever agree on every single topic in the world—even if they're best friends, loving spouses for 50 years, or Buddhist monks. There will come a time when they will have a difference of opinion. Be prepared to take the high road: agree to disagree. Opinions and perspectives are like handed-ness. A right-handed person isn't better than a left-handed person; they're just different.

ACTION MAKES THE DIFFERENCE!

No matter how much you learn, how many classes you attend, how many tutorials you take, how many books you read, the most important factor in your life is your ability to take action. Take action right now. Do it today. Don't put anything off. Even if you are afraid to fail, even if you actually DO fail, the reflection and wisdom you gain will help you grow. It's the most valuable lesson on the road to success. Take it! Do it! Grow!